SAINT BONAVENTURA

The Mind's Road to God

The Library of Liberal Arts

$ .50

The Library of Liberal Arts

OSKAR PIEST, *General Editor*

[NUMBER THIRTY-TWO]

SAINT BONAVENTURA

The Mind's Road to God

SAINT BONAVENTURA

The Mind's Road to God

Translated, with an Introduction, by

GEORGE BOAS
Professor of Philosophy, The Johns Hopkins University

THE LIBERAL ARTS PRESS
NEW YORK

Published at 153 West 72nd Street, New York 23, N. Y.

———————————

PREFACE

This translation of St. Bonaventura's *Itinerarium Mentis ad Deum* is addressed to undergraduate students of the history of philosophy who may wish to read a work of a great medieval Franciscan thinker. I have used the Latin text of the Franciscan Fathers contained in *Tria Opuscula* (Quaracchi), fifth edition, 1938. Biblical quotations are taken from the Douai Bible, since that is a translation of the Vulgate, which, it goes without saying, St. Bonaventura used. In order to make the translation more readable, I have taken the liberty of breaking up a few of the longer sentences and once in a while have inserted explanatory words and phrases in square brackets. In two places, indicated in footnotes, I have made slight emendations to the text. Students who approach this work for this first time would do well to familiarize themselves with Giotto's painting of St. Francis receiving the stigmata, for the *Itinerarium* could almost be called a meditation upon the vision there depicted.

My deepest thanks are given to the Reverend George Glanzman, S.J., who made a painstaking comparison of this translation with the Latin original and suggested several revisions which improved my first draft. I have accepted all of his suggestions gratefully but, of course, I alone am responsible for the version as it now appears. Any errors in the translation, footnotes, and introduction must be laid at my door.

G.B.

CONTENTS

BIOGRAPHICAL NOTE ON ST. BONAVENTURA

St. Bonaventura, a native of Tuscany, was born Giovanni di Fidanza in 1221. He entered the Franciscan order about 1242 and in the short space of fifteen years rose to be seventh general of that order. Professor of theology at the University of Paris, Bishop of Albano, and created a cardinal by Gregory X shortly before his death in 1274, he was widely venerated during his lifetime and is mentioned as a saint in Dante's *Paradiso*. He was canonized in 1482 by Sixtus IV and a little over a century later declared a doctor of the church by Sixtus V. He has usually been known as the Seraphic Doctor, probably because of his mysticism and constant preoccupation with the vision of the Seraph which is described in the Prologue to *The Mind's Road to God*. In addition to this little treatise, his major works are the *Reductio Artium in Theologiam* ("Reduction of the Arts to Theology"), the *Biblia Pauperum* ("Bible of the Poor"), and the *Breviloquium*.

INTRODUCTION

There should be little need of apologizing for a new translation into English of Saint Bonaventura's *Itinerarium Mentis ad Deum*, for it has been recognized by all serious historians of philosophy as one of the shorter masterpieces of medieval philosophy. It sets forth in very few pages a whole system of metaphysics; it illustrates a philosophical method; it typifies the thinking of one of the great monastic orders of the West; it stands at the beginning of Renaissance science as one of those documents in which the future can be seen in germ. Besides its importance as an outstanding work in metaphysics, a work comparable to Descartes' *Discourse on Method*, Leibniz's *Monadology*, or Hume's *Enquiry* in its compactness and suggestiveness, it represents a strain of medieval thought which has been too much neglected since the publication of *Aeterni Patris*, in 1879. That encyclical with its emphasis upon Thomism has given many people, both Catholic and non-Catholic, the impression that the philosophy of Saint Thomas Aquinas is the "official" philosophy of the Roman Catholic Church. The result of this miscomprehension has been disparagement of writings other than Thomistic. Yet even in the thirteenth century Catholic philosophers were far from being in agreement, either on matters of doctrine or method. One has only to mention such figures as Alexander of Hales, the master of Saint Bonaventura; Roger Bacon; and the various monks of Saint Victor, to realize that the confusion and disagreement which certain writers of today find in our own time were just as characteristic of a period to which they refer as one of universal concord.

The metaphysical point of view of Saint Bonaventura can

be traced back to Plotinus, if not to Philo. Fundamental to his whole system is that fusion of the three hierarchies of Neo-Platonism: the hierarchy of logical classes, that of values, and that of reality. Elementary students of logic are accustomed to the doctrine that individuals can be grouped into classes which belong to certain species; that these species are again susceptible to classification in certain genera; that these are capable of being grouped into still larger orders and families, until we come to the class which includes all other classes and which is usually called *Being*. This hierarchy of classes in the textbooks of classical logic is called the Tree of Porphyry. In non-philosophic work we find the same sort of thing illustrated in the Linnaean classification of plants and animals. The higher up one goes in this hierarchy, the more inclusive are one's classes. Thus the class of vertebrates is more inclusive than the class of mammals, and the class of animals is more inclusive than the class of vertebrates.

If we assume, as most classical writers did, that such a classification reproduces the structure of reality, that classes are ordained by God and are not simply convenient groupings made by man for his own purposes, then we can see in this order of beings a scale of creatures which might be thought of as a map of all things, a tree not only of life but of all existence. But an added assumption is usually introduced into the discussion at this point, the assumption of both Plotinus and Saint Bonaventura, that the more general a class, the more real and the better. This assumption may be argued, but one can at least imagine why someone contemplating this arrangement of classes within other classes, running from the least inclusive to the most inclusive, would maintain that there was logical priority in the more general. For before one can define, let us say, man as a rational animal, it would be necessary to know the definition of "animal"; and before one could define "animality," one would have to know the definition of "living matter." This logical order of priority and posteriority might be thought of as corresponding in some mysterious way—and it has remained mysterious to this day—to some relationship in the order of reality. The problem was to discover precisely what this relationship was.

Plotinus answered the question by the invention of a basic metaphor. The universe was subject to something which he called "emanation." The lower classes flowed out of the upper classes as light flowed from a candle. Such metaphors have been of the greatest influence in the history of thought, both philosophic and scientific. Thus we have had such figurative terms as "affinity" in chemistry, or the "life force" in biology, or the "life cycle of a nation" in history, terms which were taken literally by some people but which upon scrutiny turned out to be figures of speech. In Plotinus' case there is little doubt that he believed emanation to be literal truth; though when he came to explain how lower orders emanated from higher, he could do it only by means of a more elaborate figure of speech or by having recourse to what he thought of as a law of nature, namely, that all things produced something and that what they produced was always "lower" than they themselves. Thus, Being produced the kinds of Being, and each kind produced less inclusive kinds; and so on down to the smallest classes in which individual things were comprised.

This hierarchy of Being appears throughout the work of Saint Bonaventura, though he did not derive it immediately from Plotinus. It had become a medieval commonplace which few were willing to question. And yet he could not accept the whole theory of emanation, since he was bound by his religious faith to believe in actual creation out of nothing. The God of Plotinus was *The One* from whom everything flowed like light; the God of Saint Bonaventura was the personal God of *Genesis*. His metaphysical problem was to accommodate one to the other. This accommodation appears most clearly in the fifth chapter of the *Itinerarium*.

The second hierarchy which was fused with the logical hierarchy was that of value. There is no purely logical reason why the general should be any better than the particular, though there are good traditional grounds for thinking so. Plato, Aristotle, the Neo-Platonists, and even the Stoics had a tendency to confuse goodness with the ideal or the general. In ancient Pagan thought, there was a standard belief that no particular was ever a perfect exemplification of its class— no triangle made of matter being a perfect geometrical triangle, no human being a perfectly rational animal, no work of art a perfect realization of the artist's idea. Arguing in this way, one could see that no species would ever perfectly exemplify its genus, no genus its higher order, and so on. Hence the process "downward" from Being was degeneration. When one stops to think that the Christian religion insisted upon man's nature as having been vitiated by sin—sin which, though committed by our primordial parents, was nevertheless inherited by us—one can also see why, to a Christian, the fusion of the logical and the value-hierarchy was natural enough. We still look in vain for the perfect exemplification of animal and vegetable species, though we are inclined to believe that the species is an ideal formed for intellectual purposes, and not to be expected to exist in anything other than scientific books and articles. But to a Christian thinker of the type of Saint Bonaventura, the species and genera were the ideas of God in accordance with which He had created the world. It is they which are responsible for the orderliness of the universe; they are sometimes called by the Stoic term, *seminal reasons*. In the nineteenth century, when men were as impressed by the regularity of scientific laws as they had been in the thirteenth, people like Lord Russell found a religious satisfaction in contemplating them, the only difference being that Lord Russell did not use the Stoic term; nor did he think of scientific laws as the ideas in the mind of God. If permanence and invariability are marks of goodness, then indeed the more general the law, or the more inclusive the idea, the better. And since the most general and inclusive term is without question the term *Being*, it would follow that *Being* was the best of all things. In the sixth chapter of the *Itinerarium*, in which Saint Bonaventura discusses *Good* as the name of God, the importance of this fusion appears most clearly.

The third hierarchy, as we have said, was that of reality. In common speech we are accustomed to think of particular things in this material world of time and space as more real than ideas, or logical classes, or mathematical concepts, such as circles and triangles. We should, if untutored in the history of philosophy, think that a given man, George Washington or Abraham Lincoln, was more real than the idea of mankind, though it is doubtful whether we should proceed to maintain that the idea of "rational animal" is more real than that of "animal." The fundamental question for a philosopher is what we mean by the adjective "real" and whether we should give it a meaning such that it may be used in the comparative and superlative degrees. Saint Bonaventura was far from being unique in thinking that this adjective was comparable; indeed such modern thinkers as Hegel and his followers seemed to have taken that for granted. In any event Saint Bonaventura did believe in its comparability, and he identified the hierarchy of reality with those of logic and value.

This fusion of hierarchies lies behind the whole method of thinking which is illustrated by the *Itinerarium*, and it must be accepted by a reader who wishes to study the work sympathetically. But along with this metaphysical matrix a certain philosophical method is to be found which is of particular importance in studying this work. That method is resident in a theory of knowledge which makes true knowledge a matter of inspection, of *seeing*. We all have to believe that certain ideas must be taken for granted, whether they are the postulates of a system of geometry which we accept merely for the purpose of deducing their consequences or whether they are the simple matters of perceptual fact which we are likely to call the truths of observation. Again, when we deduce a conclusion from a set of premises, as in a simple syllogism or a bit of arithmetical reasoning, how do we know that the conclusion is not merely logically entailed in the premises, but true also to fact? Cardinal Newman, in his *Grammar of Assent*, distinguished between what he called "real assent" and "notional assent"—the former being the assent which we give to propositions of existence or, roughly, fact; the latter, that which we give to the logical conclusions. Thus the following syllogism is logically accurate, but no one would believe in the truth of its conclusion:

1. All triangles are plane figures.
2. John Doe is a triangle.
3. John Doe is a plane figure.

We should be obligated to maintain that the conclusion followed from the premises, but we would not give real assent to it nevertheless. Just what do we mean by real assent, and how does it arise?

The most obvious case of real assent occurs in the acceptance of the truths of observation. If someone is asked why he thinks sugar is sweet, he will tell you that it is because he has tasted it. If someone asks why a person believes that the sky is blue, he will be told that the person has looked and seen. Sensory observation looks like simple and direct and incontrovertible knowledge. It is not quite so simple and direct and incontrovertible as used to be thought, but we are dealing with the common-sense point of view here, and from that it has all these traits. Throughout the *Itinerarium* Saint Bonaventura emphasizes that knowledge in the last analysis comes down to seeing, to contemplation, to a kind of experience in which we know certain things to be true without further argument or demonstration. On the lowest level, this occurs in sensory observation, on the highest in the mystic vision.

Along with this insistence on direct experience as the source of all truth runs a practice which goes back at least to Philo-Judaeus in the Hebraic-Christian tradition: the practice of the allegorical method. In Philo, who was mainly interested in the Pentateuch, the allegorical method was employed in interpreting Scripture. It was believed by him that if every verse in the Bible was accepted literally, then we should have to believe things which were contrary to reason. Thus we should have to believe that God, Who is not in space, actually walked in the Garden of Eden; that He spoke as human beings speak with a physical voice; that He literally breathed into Adam the breath of life as we breathe our breath into things.[1] But to hold such beliefs is to deny the spirituality and ubiquity of God, and that is repugnant to our religious and philosophical theories. Consequently Philo maintained that these and similar texts must be interpreted allegorically, and he naturally believed that he had the key to the allegory. Similarly the *Itinerarium*, which begins as a meditation upon the vision which Saint Francis had on Mount Alverna, continues as an interpretation in philosophical terms, not only of the vision itself, but also of certain passages in Exodus and Isaiah in which details of the vision are paralleled. The Seraph which Saint Francis saw, and which had three pairs of wings, has to be interpreted as a symbol of a philosophical and religious idea. The wings become stages in the process of the mind's elevation to God, and their position on the body of the Seraph indicates the heights of the stages. Furthermore, it will be seen that even the physical world itself becomes a sort of symbol of religious ideas. This was in keeping with many traditions which were common in the Middle Ages—ideas that appeared in the Bestiaries and Lapidaries, and which we retain in weakened form in some of our pseudoheraldic symbols, such as the Eagle, the Lion, and the Olive Branch; or the use of certain colors, such as blue for hope, white for purity, red for passion. Among these more popular symbols was that of the macrocosm and the microcosm, according to which a human being exactly mirrored the universe as a whole, so that one could pass from one to the other and find corresponding parts and functions. Much of this was undoubtedly fortified by Saint Francis' fashion of humanizing natural objects—the sun, the birds, the rain, and so on—in his talks and poems. Few, if any, of the saints seem to have felt such an intimate relationship with

---

[1] The student will do well to read Philo's *Allegorical Interpretation* for examples of his method. The most readily available translation is that of G. H. Whitaker in the Loeb Library. For a thorough study of the whole matter, he should consult H. A. Wolfson's *Philo* (Cambridge: Harvard University, 1949).

the physical world as the founder of the Order to which Saint Bonaventura belonged.

The full effect of this appears in the first chapter of the *Itinerarium*, in which we are told that God may be seen in His traces in the physical world. This is the basis of what sometimes is called natural theology; for if we can actually see the traces of God about us in the order of natural law, then we have a start toward knowledge of the divine mind which is sure. It is only a start, Saint Bonaventura maintains, but it is the proper start. It means that one does not have to be a great rationalist, an erudite theologian, a *doctor*, to know religious truths. One has only to look about one and observe that certain laws obtain; that there is order; that all things are "disposed in weight, number, and measure." This can be *seen*; and when it is seen, one has a reflection of the divine mind in one's sensory experience. One has only to contrast this with the method of Saint Thomas Aquinas in the *Summa Theologica*, in which God's existence is proved by a series of rational arguments—where objections are analyzed, authorities are consulted and weighed, multiple distinctions are made, and the whole emphasis is upon reason rather than observation. Saint Bonaventura seems to have as his purpose a demonstration of God's existence and of His traits which is not irrational but nonrational. That is, he would be far from saying that his conclusions would not stand up under rational criticism, but would insist that his method, to use modern language, is empirical rather than rational. To take a trivial example from another field, we could prove that a person had committed a crime either by circumstantial evidence or by direct testimony. If we can produce two or three persons who actually saw him commit the crime, we do not feel that we must corroborate what they say by a rational demonstration that he could have committed it, that he had a motive for committing it, that he threatened to commit it, that no one else could have committed it, and so on. We like to think that a good case gives us both kinds of evidence, but frequently we have to be satisfied with one type or bits of both types. Saint

Bonaventura might be compared to the man who insists on direct testimony; Saint Thomas to him who puts his trust exclusively in circumstantial evidence, though the comparison would be superficial. It would be superficial since both would agree that God's existence could be shown in both ways.

The method of direct observation by which one is made certain of one's beliefs leads step by step to the mystic vision. The mystic, like the strict empiricist, has a kind of knowledge which is indisputable. No one can deny what the mystic sees any more than one can deny what the sensory observer sees. The philosopher who bases all knowledge upon the direct observation of colors, sounds, shapes, and so on, has knowledge which he readily admits is uncommunicable, in spite of the fact that most of us use words for our elementary sensations in the same ways. But whether John Doe, who is looking upon a patch of red, sees precisely what Richard Roe sees, could be doubted and has been doubted. For the psychological equipment, the sensory apparatus of the two men may and probably does contribute something to even the most simple sensory experiences. If Messrs. Doe and Roe are exactly alike in all relevant ways, then one may reasonably conclude that their sensations are exactly alike. But nevertheless Roe would not be having Doe's sensation, for each man is the terminus of causal events which diverge from a given point and which cease to be identical once they have entered the human body. Thus a bell may be ringing and therefore giving off air waves. When these air waves enter the body of Roe, they are no longer the same waves which have entered the body of Doe; for Roe's auditory nerves, no matter how similar to Doe's, are not existentially identical with them. If we distinguish between existential and qualitative identity, and we all do, then we may say that Doe and Roe have qualitatively identical but existentially nonidentical sensations. Until Roe can hear with Doe's ears and auditory nerves and auditory brain centers, he will never experience Doe's auditory sensations. Similarly with the mystic vision. If one man has such a vision, he is not made uneasy by the fact that another does not have it. The

other man has only to follow the discipline which will lead
him to it. Saint Bonaventura traces the steps on this road, one
by one, until he reaches his goal.

The mysticism of Saint Bonaventura was peculiar in that it
was based on a theory of knowledge in which all degrees of
knowledge were similarly direct, immediate, and nonrational.
One sees God's traces in the sensory world; one sees His image
in the mind; one sees His goodness in human goodness; one
sees His powers in the operations of our own powers—it is always a question of direct seeing. Thus we have the possibility
of real, rather than notional, assent in all fields of knowledge.
We are not forced to know *about* things; we can know *them*.
We have, to use other familiar terms, direct acquaintance with,
rather than descriptions of, them. In other words, there is never
any real need for rational discourse, for erudition. The simplest man of good will can see God as clearly as the most
learned scholar. That made a philosophy such as this a perfect
instrument for the Christian, for throughout the Christian
tradition ran a current of anti-intellectualism. Christianity was
held to be a religion, not merely a body of abstract knowledge.
It was an experience as well as a theory. A man of faith could
have as certain knowledge of God as the man of learning. This
did not discourage the Christian from attempting to build up
rational systems which would demonstrate to the world of
scholars what the religious man knew by faith. Far from it.
But what Kant was to say of the relationship between concepts
and precepts, the Christian could have said of that between
faith and reason, or religion and philosophy: faith without
reason is blind, reason without faith empty.

The difficulty with the extremists who maintained that
either one or the other faculty was sufficient was that faith
and reason were both supposed to assert something. Whether
you believed by faith or by reason, you believed in ideas which
presumably made sense, could be stated in words, could be
true or false. If you believed in one of these truths by faith,
without reason, you were in the position of a man who had
no knowledge of what he was believing nor why, nor even

whether there was any good reason for believing in it rather than its contradictory. It was all very well for a man like Tertullian to maintain that there was more glory in believing something irrational—inept—than in believing something demonstrably true. Most Christian philosophers were anxious to put a sound rational underpinning beneath their beliefs. Similarly, if you had only rational knowledge, you were like a blind man who might be convinced that there were such things as colors, analogous to sounds and odors, but who had no direct acquaintance with them; or again like a man who had read an eloquent description of a great painting, but who had never seen it. Though all Christians were in the position of maintaining that there were some beliefs, those in the mysteries, which could not be rationally demonstrated, nevertheless they all, including Saint Bonaventura, pushed their rational demonstrations as far as they were able. Thus Saint Bonaventura goes so far as to attempt a dialectical proof of the dogma of the Trinity (Ch. VI), though he realizes that such a proof is not sufficient for religion.

It is worth pointing out that Franciscan philosophy as a whole tended to put more emphasis upon the observation of the natural world than its great rival, Thomism, did. Even in the *Little Flowers* of Saint Francis, only in a remote sense of the word a philosophical work, there is a fondness for what we call Nature which led him at times close to heresy. Later there were Franciscans like Roger Bacon, Duns Scotus, and their great friend and protector, Robert Grosseteste, whose interest in what we would call science, as distinct from philosophy, was almost their main interest. Indeed, one might without too much exaggeration maintain that the impetus to the study of the natural world through empirical methods came from the Franciscans. This appears in the early chapters of the *Itinerarium*, where observational science becomes not simply the satisfaction of idle curiosity, but the fulfillment of a religious obligation. But it goes without saying that a man of science may discover truths which contradict what he has believed on faith and that a man of faith may look to science, not for everything which it is capable of revealing, but only for those things which corroborate his faith. The best illustration of this conflict is found in the use made of arithmetic by allegorists, as early as Philo. Few mathematicians today would play upon the curious properties of numbers—virgin numbers, perfect numbers, superabundant numbers, numbers which are the sums of such numbers as *three* and *four*—to prove religious truths. Few men of religion would, I imagine, seek validation of their religious beliefs in the properties of numbers, finding it extraordinary that there are four Gospels, four points of the compass, four winds, four elements (earth, water, air, and fire), four seasons, four humors, four temperaments. But all men will usually feel uneasy in the presence of contradiction and will do their best to bring all their beliefs into harmony with one another. The question reduces to the motivation of knowledge, the question of why exploration is pushed into fields which previously have been *terrae incognitae*. And when one compares science as it was before the fourteenth century and that which it became after that date, one sees that only a strong emotional propulsion would have produced the change of interest. That propulsion, we are suggesting, came from the Franciscans.

The student who has no acquaintance with the philosophy of Saint Bonaventura can do no better than to begin with the *Itinerarium*. It is short and yet complete; it is typical of his manner of thinking; and it presents only the difficulties which any medieval philosophical text presents. There is no need to hack one's way through a jungle of authorities, quotations, refutations, distinctions, and textual exegeses. It is not a commentary on another man's book; it is a straightforward statement of a philosophical point of view. It illustrates the manner in which its author's contemporaries and predecessors utilized Biblical texts, and it also illustrates the knowledge of physics and psychology which was current in the thirteenth century. It is thus one of those representative documents which it behooves all students of intellectual history to know. It should be read with sympathy. One should accept its author's various assumptions, both methodological and doctrinal, and begin from there. There would be no point in trying to translate it in terms of the twentieth century, for the attempt would fail. But similarly one would not attempt to translate Dante's cosmology into modern terms nor justify Chartres Cathedral in terms of functional architecture as that is understood by modern engineers. This book is a kind of prose poem, with a dramatic development of its own as one rises from step to step toward a mystic vision of God. That would seem to be the best approach which the beginner could make to it.

GEORGE BOAS

THE JOHNS HOPKINS UNIVERSITY
July, 1953

SELECTED BIBLIOGRAPHY

St. Bonaventura, *Breviloquium,* tr. by Erwin Esser Nemmers, St. Louis and London, 1946.

————, *Opera Omnia,* As Claras Aquas (Quaracchi), 10 vols., 1937.

Dady, Sister Mary Rachael, *The Theory of Knowledge of St. Bonaventura,* Washington, D. C., 1939.

De Benedictis, Matthew M., *The Social Thought of St. Bonaventura.* Washington, D. C., 1946.

Gilson, E. H., *La Philosophie de St. Bonaventure,* Paris, 1924.

Healy, Sister Emma Thérèse, *Saint Bonaventura's De reductione artium ad theologiam* (commentary with introduction and translation), St. Bonaventura, N. Y., 1939.

Prentice, Robert P., *The Psychology of Love According to St. Bonaventura,* St. Bonaventura, N. Y., 1951.

THE MIND'S ROAD TO GOD

PROLOGUE

1. To begin with, the first principle from Whom all illumination descends as from the Father of Light, by Whom are given all the best and perfect gifts [James, 1, 17], the eternal Father do I call upon through His Son, our Lord Jesus Christ, that by the intercession of the most holy Virgin Mary, mother of God Himself and of our Lord, Jesus Christ, and of the blessed Francis, our father and leader, He may enlighten the eyes of our mind to guide our feet into the way of that peace "which surpasses all understanding" [Eph., 1, 17; Luke, 1, 79; Phil., 4, 7], which peace our Lord Jesus Christ has announced and given to us; which lesson our father Francis always taught, in all of whose preaching was the annunciation of peace both in the beginning and in the end, wishing for peace in every greeting, yearning for ecstatic peace in every moment of contemplation, as a citizen of that Jerusalem of which that man of peace said, with those that hated peace he was peaceable [Ps., 119, 7], "Pray ye for the things that are for the peace of Jerusalem" [Ps., 121, 6]. For he knew that the throne of Solomon was nowise save in peace, since it is written, "His place is in peace and His abode in Sion" [Ps., 75, 3].

2. Since, then, following the example of the most blessed father Francis, I breathlessly sought this peace, I, a sinner, who have succeeded to the place of that most blessed father after his death, the seventh Minister General of the brothers, though in all ways unworthy—it happened that by the divine will in the thirty-third year after the death of that blessed man I ascended to Mount Alverna as to a quiet place, with the desire of seeking spiritual peace; and staying there, while I meditated on the ascent of the mind to God, amongst other things there occurred that miracle which happened in the same place to the blessed Francis himself, the vision namely

of the winged Seraph in the likeness of the Crucified. While looking upon this vision, I immediately saw that it signified the suspension of our father himself in contemplation and the way by which he came to it.

3. For by those six wings are rightly to be understood the six stages of illumination by which the soul, as if by steps or progressive movements, was disposed to pass into peace by ecstatic elevations of Christian wisdom. The way, however, is only through the most burning love of the Crucified, Who so transformed Paul, "caught up into the third heaven" [II Cor., 12, 2], into Christ, that he said, "With Christ I am nailed to the cross, yet I live, now not I, but Christ liveth in me" [Gal., 2, 19]; who therefore so absorbed the mind of Francis that his soul was manifest in his flesh and he bore the most holy stigmata of the Passion in his body for two years before his death. Therefore the symbol of the six-winged Seraph signifies the six stages of illumination, which begin with God's creatures and lead up to God, to Whom no one can enter properly save through the Crucified. For he who does not enter by the door but otherwise, he is a thief and a robber [John, 10, 1]. But if anyone does enter by this door, he shall go in and go out and shall find pastures [John, 9]. Because of this John says in his Apocalypse [22, 14], "Blessed are they that wash their robes in the blood of the Lamb, that they may have a right to the Tree of Life and may enter in by the gates into the City"; as if he were to say that one cannot enter into the heavenly Jerusalem through contemplation unless one enter through the blood of the Lamb as through a gate. For one is not disposed to contemplation which leads to mental eleva-tion unless one be with Daniel a man of desires [Dan., 9, 23]. But desires are kindled in us in two ways: by the cry of prayer, which makes one groan with the murmuring of one's heart, and by a flash of apprehension by which the mind turns most directly and intensely to the rays of light [Ps., 37, 9].

4. Therefore to the cry of prayer through Christ crucified, by Whose blood we are purged of the filth of vice, do I first invite the reader, lest perchance he should believe that it suf-

fices to read without unction, speculate without devotion, investigate without wonder, examine without exultation, work without piety, know without love, understand without humility, be zealous without divine grace, see without wisdom divinely inspired. Therefore to those predisposed by divine grace, to the humble and the pious, to those filled with compunction and devotion, anointed with the oil of gladness [Ps., 44, 8], to the lovers of divine wisdom, inflamed with desire for it, to those wishing to give themselves over to praising God, to wondering over Him and to delighting in Him, do I propose the following reflections, hinting that little or nothing is the outer mirror unless the mirror of the mind be clear and polished.

Bestir yourself then, O man of God, you who previously resisted the pricks of conscience, before you raise your eyes to the rays of wisdom shining in that mirror, lest by chance you fall into the lower pit of shadows from the contemplation of those rays.

5. I have decided to divide my treatise into seven chapters, heading them with titles so that their contents may be the more easily understood. I ask therefore that one think rather of the intention of the writer than of his work, of the sense of the words rather than the rude speech, of truth rather than beauty, of the exercise of the affections rather than the erudition of the intellect. That such may come about, the progress of these thoughts must not be perused lightly, but should be meditated upon in greatest deliberation.

THE MENDICANT'S VISION IN THE WILDERNESS

CHAPTER ONE

OF THE STAGES IN THE ASCENT TO GOD AND OF HIS REFLECTION IN HIS TRACES IN THE UNIVERSE [1]

1. Blessed is the man whose help is from Thee. In his heart he hath disposed to ascend by steps, in the vale of tears, in the place which he hath set [Ps., 83, 6]. Since beatitude is nothing else than the fruition of the highest good, and the highest good is above us, none can be made blessed unless he ascend above himself, not by the ascent of his body but by that of his heart. But we cannot be raised above ourselves except by a higher power raising us up. For howsoever the interior steps are disposed, nothing is accomplished unless it is accompanied by divine aid. Divine help, however, comes to those who seek it from their hearts humbly and devoutly; and this means to sigh for it in this vale of tears, aided only by fervent prayer. Thus prayer is the mother and source of ascent

[1] I have translated the Latin *speculatio,* which appears over and over again in this work, in a variety of ways. St. Bonaventura plays upon its various shades of meaning—*reflection, speculation, consideration*—for he seems haunted by the basic metaphor of the universe's being a sort of mirror (*speculum*) in which God is to be seen. The Italian and French translators have the advantage of those of us who write English, for they have merely to transliterate the Latin word. We have a similar difficulty in the Latin word *vestigia,* which I have translated *traces.* It will hardly do to write *vestiges* or *footprints,* and *traces* is not much better. St. Bonaventura simply means that by considering the work of art one will know the artist. His handiwork shows traces of his workmanship. But we are likely to think of traces as something which are left behind, whereas God is not to be thought of as having created the world and then left it alone, as Pascal said of Descartes' God.

(*sursum-actionis*) in God. Therefore Dionysius, in his book, *Mystical Theology* [ch. 1, 1], wishing to instruct us in mental elevation, prefaces his work by prayer. Therefore let us pray and say to the Lord our God, "Conduct me, O Lord, in Thy way, and I will walk in Thy truth; let my heart rejoice that it may fear Thy name" [Ps., 85, 11].

2. By praying thus one is enlightened about the knowledge of the stages in the ascension to God. For since, relative to our life on earth, the world is itself a ladder for ascending to God, we find here certain traces [of His hand], certain images, some corporeal, some spiritual, some temporal, some aeviternal; consequently some outside us, some inside. That we may arrive at an understanding of the First Principle, which is most spiritual and eternal and above us, we ought to proceed through the traces which are corporeal and temporal and outside us; and this is to be led into the way of God. We ought next to enter into our minds, which are the eternal image of God, spiritual and internal; and this is to walk in the truth of God. We ought finally to pass over into that which is eternal, most spiritual, and above us, looking to the First Principle; and this is to rejoice in the knowledge of God and in the reverence of His majesty.

3. Now this is the three days' journey into the wilderness [Ex., 3, 18]; this is the triple illumination of one day, first as the evening, second as the morning, third as noon; this signifies the threefold existence of things, as in matter, in [creative] intelligence, and in eternal art, wherefore it is said, *Be it made, He made it,* and *It was so done* [Gen., 1]; and this also means the triple substance in Christ, Who is our ladder, namely, the corporeal, the spiritual, and the divine.

4. Following this threefold progress, our mind has three principal aspects. One refers to the external body, wherefore it is called animality or sensuality; the second looks inward and into itself, wherefore it is called spirit; the third looks above itself, wherefore it is called mind. From all of which considerations it ought to be so disposed for ascending as a whole into God that it may love Him with all its mind, with

all its heart, and with all its soul [Mark, 12, 30]. And in this consists both the perfect observance of the Law and Christian wisdom.

5. Since, however, all of the aforesaid modes are twofold—as when we consider God as the alpha and omega, or in so far as we happen to see God in one of the aforesaid modes as *through* a mirror and *in* a mirror, or as one of those considerations can be mixed with the other conjoined to it or may be considered alone in its purity—hence it is necessary that these three principal stages become sixfold, so that as God made the world in six days and rested on the seventh, so the microcosm by six successive stages of illumination is led in the most orderly fashion to the repose of contemplation. As a symbol of this we have the six steps to the throne of Solomon [III Kings, 10, 19]; the Seraphim whom Isaiah saw have six wings; after six days the Lord called Moses out of the midst of the cloud [Ex., 24, 16]; and Christ after six days, as is said in Matthew [17, 1], brought His disciples up into a mountain and was transfigured before them.

6. Therefore, according to the six stages of ascension into God, there are six stages of the soul's powers by which we mount from the depths to the heights, from the external to the internal, from the temporal to the eternal—to wit, sense, imagination, reason, intellect, intelligence, and the apex of the mind, the illumination of conscience (*Synteresis*). These stages are implanted in us by nature, deformed by sin, reformed by grace, to be purged by justice, exercised by knowledge, perfected by wisdom.

7. Now at the Creation, man was made fit for the repose of contemplation, and therefore God placed him in a paradise of delight [Gen., 2, 16]. But turning himself away from the true light to mutable goods, he was bent over by his own sin, and the whole human race by original sin, which doubly infected human nature, ignorance infecting man's mind and concupiscence his flesh. Hence man, blinded and bent, sits in the shadows and does not see the light of heaven unless grace with justice succor him from concupiscence, and knowledge with

wisdom against ignorance. All of which is done through Jesus Christ, Who of God is made unto us wisdom and justice and sanctification and redemption [I Cor., 1, 30]. He is the virtue and wisdom of God, the Word incarnate, the author of grace and truth—that is, He has infused the grace of charity, which, since it is from a pure heart and good conscience and unfeigned faith, rectifies the whole soul in the threefold way mentioned above. He has taught the knowledge of the truth according to the triple mode of theology—that is, the symbolic, the literal, and the mystical—so that by the symbolic we may make proper use of sensible things, by the literal we may properly use the intelligible, and by the mystical we may be carried aloft to supermental levels.

8. Therefore he who wishes to ascend to God must, avoiding sin, which deforms nature, exercise the above-mentioned natural powers for regenerating grace, and do this through prayer. He must strive toward purifying justice, and this in intercourse; toward the illumination of knowledge, and this in meditation; toward the perfection of wisdom, and this in contemplation. Now just as no one comes to wisdom save through grace, justice, and knowledge, so none comes to contemplation save through penetrating meditation, holy conversation, and devout prayer. Just as grace is the foundation of the will's rectitude and of the enlightenment of clear and penetrating reason, so, first, we must pray; secondly, we must live holily; thirdly, we must strive toward the reflection of truth and, by our striving, mount step by step until we come to the high mountain where we shall see the God of gods in Sion [Ps., 83, 8].

9. Since, then, we must mount Jacob's ladder before descending it, let us place the first rung of the ascension in the depths, putting the whole sensible world before us as a mirror, by which ladder we shall mount up to God, the Supreme Creator, that we may be true Hebrews crossing from Egypt to the land promised to our fathers; let us be Christians crossing with Christ from this world over to the Father [John, 13, 1]; let us also be lovers of wisdom, which calls to us and

says, "Come over to me, all ye that desire me, and be filled with my fruits" [Ecclesiasticus, 24, 26]. For by the greatness of the beauty and of the creature, the Creator of them may be seen [Wisdom, 13, 5].

10. There shine forth, however, the Creator's supreme power and wisdom and benevolence in created things, as the carnal sense reports trebly to the inner sense. For the carnal sense serves him who either understands rationally or believes faithfully or contemplates intellectually. Contemplating, it considers the actual existence of things; believing, it considers the habitual course of things; reasoning, it considers the potential excellence of things.

11. In the first mode, the aspect of one contemplating, considering things in themselves, sees in them weight, number, and measure [Wisdom, 11, 21]—weight, which directs things to a certain location; [2] number, by which they are distinguished from one another; and measure, by which they are limited. And so one sees in them mode, species, and order; and also substance, power, and operation. From these one can rise as from the traces to understanding the power, wisdom, and immense goodness of the Creator.

12. In the second mode, the aspect of a believer considering this world, one reaches its origin, course, and terminus. For by faith we believe that the ages are fashioned by the Word of Life [Hebr., 11, 3]; by faith we believe that the ages of the three laws—that is, the ages of the law of Nature, of Scripture, and of Grace—succeed each other and occur in most orderly fashion; by faith we believe that the world will be ended at the last judgment—taking heed of the power in the first, of the providence in the second, of the justice of the most high principle in the third.

13. In the third mode, the aspect of one inquiring rationally, one sees that some things merely are; others, however, are and live; others, finally, are, live, and discern. And the first are lesser things, the second midway, and the third the best.

---

[2] Reading *pondus quo ad situm,* instead of *quoad.*

Again, one sees that some are only corporeal, others partly corporeal and partly spiritual, from which it follows that some are entirely spiritual and are better and more worthy than either of the others. One sees, nonetheless, that some are mutable and corruptible, as earthly things; others mutable and incorruptible, as celestial things, from which it follows that some are immutable and incorruptible, as the supercelestial things.

From these visible things, therefore, one mounts to considering the power and wisdom and goodness of God as being, living, and understanding; purely spiritual and incorruptible and immutable.

14. This consideration, however, is extended according to the sevenfold condition of creatures, which is a sevenfold testimony to the divine power, wisdom, and goodness, as one considers the origin, magnitude, multitude, beauty, plenitude, operation, and order of all things. For the *origin* of things, according to their creation, distinction, and beauty, in the work of the six days indicates the divine power producing all things from nothing, wisdom distinguishing all things clearly, and goodness adorning all things generously. *Magnitude* of things, either according to the measure of their length, width, and depth, or according to the excellence of power spreading itself in length, breadth, and depth, as appears in the diffusion of light, or again according to the efficacy of its inner, continuous, and diffused operation, as appears in the operation of fire—magnitude, I say, indicates manifestly the immensity of the power, wisdom, and goodness of the triune God, Who exists unlimited in all things through His power, presence, and essence. *Multitude* of things, according to the diversity of genus, species, and individuality, in substance, form, or figure, and efficacy beyond all human estimation, clearly indicates and shows the immensity of the aforesaid traits in God. *Beauty* of things, according to the variety of light, figure, and color in bodies simple and mixed and even composite, as in the celestial bodies, minerals, stones and metals, plants and animals, obviously proclaims the three mentioned traits. *Pleni-*

tude of things—according to which matter is full of forms because of the seminal reasons; form is full of power because of its activity; power is full of effects because of its efficiency—declares the same manifestly. *Operation,* multiplex inasmuch as it is natural, artificial, and moral, by its very variety shows the immensity of that power, art, and goodness which indeed are in all things the cause of their being, the principle of their intelligibility, and the order of their living. *Order,* by reason of duration, situation, and influence, as prior and posterior, upper and lower, nobler and less noble, indicates clearly in the book of creation the primacy, sublimity, and dignity of the First Principle in relation to its infinite power. The order of the divine laws, precepts, and judgments in the Book of Scripture indicates the immensity of His wisdom. The order of the divine sacraments, rewards, and punishments in the body of the Church indicates the immensity of His goodness. Hence order leads us most obviously into the first and highest, most powerful, wisest, and best.

15. He, therefore, who is not illumined by such great splendor of created things is blind; he who is not awakened by such great clamor is deaf; he who does not praise God because of all these effects is dumb; he who does not note the First Principle from such great signs is foolish. Open your eyes therefore, prick up your spiritual ears, open your lips, and apply your heart, that you may see your God in all creatures, may hear Him, praise Him, love and adore Him, magnify and honor Him, lest the whole world rise against you. For on this account the whole world will fight against the unwise [Prov., 5, 21]; but to the wise will there be matter for pride, who with the Prophet can say, "Thou hast given me, O Lord, a delight in Thy doings: and in the works of Thy hands I shall rejoice [Ps., 91, 5]. . . . How great are Thy works, O Lord; Thou hast made all things in wisdom; the earth is filled with Thy riches" [Ps., 103, 24].

CHAPTER TWO

Of the Reflection of God in His Traces in the Sensible World

1. But since with respect to the mirror of sensible things it happens that God is contemplated not only *through* them, as by His traces, but also *in* them, in so far as He is in them by essence, potency, and presence; and to consider this is higher than the preceding; therefore a consideration of this sort holds next place as a second step in contemplation, by which we should be led to the contemplation of God in all creatures which enter into our minds through the bodily senses.

2. Let it be noted then that this world, which is called the "macrocosm," enters our souls, which are called the "microcosm," through the doors of the five senses, according to the apprehension, delectation, and judgment of sensible things themselves. This is apparent as follows: In the world some things are generating, some generated, some governing the former and the latter. The generating are simple bodies, celestial bodies, and the four elements. For from the elements, by virtue of the light which reconciles the contrariety of elements in mixtures, there can be generated and produced whatsoever things are generated and produced through the operation of a natural power. But the generated are bodies composed of the elements, like minerals, vegetables, sensible things, and human bodies. The rulers of the former and the latter are spiritual substances, either conjoined entirely, as are the animal souls; or conjoined though separable, as are the rational spirits; or entirely separated, as are the celestial spirits, which philosophers call "intelligences," but we "angels." These, according to the philosophers, move the celestial

bodies; and thus there is attributed to them the administration of the universe by taking over from the First Cause, that is God, their active influence, which they pour out in accordance with the work of governing, which looks to the natural harmony of things. According to the theologians, however, there is attributed to them the rule of the universe in accordance with the power of the supreme God with respect to the work of reparation, wherefore they are called "ministering spirits," sent to minister to them who shall receive the inheritance of salvation [Hebr., 1, 14].

3. Therefore, man, who is called a "microcosm," has five senses like five doors, through which enters into his soul the cognition of all that is in the sensible world. For through sight enter the transparent (*sublimia*) [1], luminous, and other colored bodies; through touch the solid and terrestrial bodies; by the three intermediate senses the intermediates, as by taste the aqueous, by hearing the aerial, by odor the vaporous—all of which have something of a humid nature, something aerial, something fiery or warm, as appears in the smoke which is freed from incense.

There enter then through these doors, not only simple bodies, but also composite, mixed from these. But since by sense we perceive not only these particular sensibles, which are light, sound, odor, savor, and the four primary qualities which touch apprehends, but also the common sensibles, which are number, magnitude, figure, rest, and motion, and since everything which is moved is moved by something, and some are self-moved and remain at rest, as the animals, it follows that when through these five senses we apprehend the motion of bodies, we are led to the cognition of spiritual movers, as through an effect we are led to a knowledge of its causes.

[1] This may be a mistranslation. For St. Bonaventura may be talking about our perception of the heavenly bodies. Since, however, he is listing the three kinds of visible objects, one of which is clearly luminous, and since the heavenly bodies are luminous, he must be speaking of some kind of visible object which is not luminous. *Sublime* in classical Latin was used for the air, and this usage survives in the English verb, *sublimate*, "to vaporize."

4. As far as the three kinds of things are concerned, this whole sensible world enters into the human soul through *apprehension*. The external sensibles, however, are what first enter the soul through the five doors of the senses. They enter, I say, not through their substance, but through their similitudes. These are first generated in the medium, and from the medium are generated in the organ and pass from the external organ into the internal, and from there into the apprehensive power. And thus the generation of the [sensible] species in the medium and from the medium into the organ and the reaction of the apprehensive power to it [the species] produce the apprehension of all those things which the soul apprehends from without.

5. Upon this apprehension, if it be of the appropriate thing, there follows *delight*. Sense, however, takes delight in an object perceived through an abstracted similitude either by reason of its beauty, as in sight; or by reason of its agreeableness, as in odor and hearing; or by reason of wholesomeness, as in taste and touch, speaking with appropriation.[2] All delight, however, is by reason of proportion. But since a species is form, power, and operation, according to whether it is thought of as related to the principle from which it comes, to the medium through which it passes, or to the end for which it acts, therefore proportion may be considered in similitude, inasmuch as it is a species or form and thus is called *speciositas* [beauty], because beauty is nothing other than numerical equality or a certain relation of parts with agreeable color. Or else proportion may be considered as potency or power, and thus it is called "suavity," for active power does not exceed immoderately the powers of the recipient,

[2] This is a technical term which is used when one appropriates to a function what is really a trait of that which possesses the function. Thus if a whole person has five senses, he touches as a whole, sees as a whole, and exercises all his other senses as a whole. But we can speak of his sight doing the seeing, his taste doing the smelling, and so on. This becomes of importance when a Catholic theologian speaks of the Father as creating the world, whereas he believes that all three persons of the Trinity are always present in all the acts of the Trinity.

since the senses are pained by extremes and delight in the mean. Or it may be considered, by thinking of species, as efficacy and impression, which is proportional when the agent by impression supplies what the recipient lacks; and this is to save and nourish it, which appears especially in taste and touch. And thus through delight the external pleasures enter into the soul by similitudes in a triple mode of delighting.

6. After the delight of apprehension comes *judgment*. By this we not only judge whether something is white or black, for this pertains to a special sense, not only whether it is healthful or harmful, for this pertains to the inner sense, but also why something is delightful. And in this act the question is raised about the reasons for our delight which sense derives from the object. This happens when we ask why something is beautiful, pleasant, and wholesome. And it is discovered that the answer is equality of proportion. Equality, however, is the same in the great and the small, and is not spread out through a thing's dimensions; nor does it change and pass away when there is alteration through change or motion. Therefore it abstracts from place, time, and motion, and thus is unchangeable, illimitable, without ends, and in all ways spiritual. Judgment is, therefore, an action which causes the sensible species, received sensibly through sense, to enter the intellective faculty by purification and abstraction. And thus the whole world can enter into the human soul through the doors of the senses by the three aforesaid operations.

7. These all, however, are traces in which we can see the reflection of our God. For since the apprehended species is a likeness produced in the medium and then impressed upon the organ itself, and by means of that impression leads to its principle and source—that is to say, to the object of knowledge—manifestly it follows that the eternal light generates out of itself a likeness or coequal radiance which is consubstantial and coeternal. And He Who is the image and likeness of the invisible God [Col., 1, 15] and "the brightness of His glory and the figure of His substance" [Hebr., 1, 3], He Who is everywhere through His primal generation, as an

object generates its likeness in the whole medium, is united by the grace of union to an individual of rational nature— as a species to a corporeal organ—so that by that union He may lead us back to the Father as to the primordial source and object. If then all knowable things can generate their likeness (*species*), obviously they proclaim that in them as in a mirror can be seen the eternal generation of the Word, the Image, and the Son, eternally emanating from God the Father.

8. In this way the species, delighting us as beautiful, pleasant, and wholesome, implies that in that first species is the primal beauty, pleasure, and wholesomeness in which is the highest proportionality and equality to the generator. In this is power, not through imagination, but entering our minds through the truth of apprehension. Here is impression, salubrious and satisfying, and expelling all lack in the apprehending mind. If, then, delight is the conjunction of the harmonious, and the likeness of God alone is the most highly beautiful, pleasant, and wholesome, and if it is united in truth and in inwardness and in plenitude which employs our entire capacity, obviously it can be seen that in God alone is the original and true delight, and that we are led back to seeking it from all other delights.

9. By a more excellent and immediate way are we led by judgment into seeing eternal truths more surely. For if judgment comes about through the reason's abstracting from place, time, and change, and therefore from dimension, succession, and transmutation, by the immutable, illimitable, and endless reason, and if there is nothing immutable, illimitable, and endless except the eternal, then all which is eternal is God or is in God. If, then, all things of which we have more certain judgments are judged by this mode of reasoning, it is clear that this is the reason of all things and the infallible rule and light of truth, in which all things shine forth infallibly, indestructibly, indubitably, irrefragably, unquestionably, unchangeably, boundlessly, endlessly, indivisibly, and intellectually. And therefore those laws by which we make certain judgments concerning all sensible things which

come into our consideration—since they [the laws] are infallible and indubitable rules of the apprehending intellect—are indelibly stored up in the memory as if always present, are irrefragable and unquestionable rules of the judging intellect. And this is so because, as Augustine says [*Lib. Arb.,* II, ch. 4], no one judges these things except by these rules. It must thus be true that they are incommutable and incorruptible since they are necessary, and boundless since they are illimitable, endless since eternal. Therefore they must be indivisible since intellectual and incorporeal, not made but uncreated, eternally existing in eternal art, by which, through which, and in accordance with which all things possessing form are formed. Neither, therefore, can we judge with certainty except through that which was not only the form producing all things but also the preserver of all and the distinguisher of all, as the being who preserves the form in all things, the directing rule by which our mind judges all things which enter into it through the senses.

10. This observation is extended by a consideration of the seven different kinds of number by which, as if by seven steps, we ascend to God. Augustine shows this in his book *On the True Religion* and in the sixth book *On Music,* wherein he assigns the differences of the numbers as they mount step by step from sensible things to the Maker of all things, so that God may be seen in all.

For he says that numbers are in bodies and especially in sounds and words, and he calls these *sonorous.* Some are abstracted from these and received into our senses, and these he calls *heard.* Some proceed from the soul into the body, as appears in gestures and bodily movements, and these he calls *uttered.* Some are in the pleasures of the senses which arise from attending to the species which have been received, and these he calls *sensual.* Some are retained in the memory, and these he calls *remembered.* Some are the bases of our judgments about all these, and these he calls *judicial,* which, as has been said above, necessarily transcend our minds because they are infallible and incontrovertible. By these there are imprinted on our minds the *artificial* numbers which Augustine does not include in this classification because they are connected with the judicial numbers from which flow the uttered numbers out of which are created the numerical forms of those things made by art. Hence, from the highest through the middle to the lowest, there is an ordered descent. Thence do we ascend step by step from the sonorous numbers by means of the uttered, the sensual, and the remembered.

Since, therefore, all things are beautiful and in some way delightful, and beauty and delight do not exist apart from proportion, and proportion is primarily in number, it needs must be that all things are rhythmical (*numerosa*). And for this reason number is the outstanding exemplar in the mind of the Maker, and in things it is the outstanding trace leading to wisdom. Since this is most evident to all and closest to God, it leads most directly to God as if by the seven differentiae. It causes Him to be known in all corporeal and sensible things while we apprehend the rhythmical, delight in rhythmical proportions, and through the laws of rhythmical proportions judge irrefragably.

11. From these two initial steps by which we are led to seeing God in His traces, as if we had two wings falling to our feet, we can determine that all creatures of this sensible world lead the mind of the one contemplating and attaining wisdom to the eternal God; for they are shadows, echoes, and pictures, the traces, simulacra, and reflections of that First Principle most powerful, wisest, and best; of that light and plenitude; of that art productive, exemplifying, and ordering, given to us for looking upon God. They are signs divinely bestowed which, I say, are exemplars or rather exemplifications set before our yet untrained minds, limited to sensible things, so that through the sensibles which they see they may be carried forward to the intelligibles which they do not see, as if by signs to the signified.

12. The creatures of this sensible world signify the invisible things of God [Rom., 1, 20], partly because God is of all creation the origin, exemplar, and end, and because every

effect is the sign of its cause, the exemplification of the exemplar, and the way to the end to which it leads; partly from its proper representation; partly from prophetic prefiguration; partly from angelic operation; partly from further ordination. For every creature is by nature a sort of picture and likeness of that eternal wisdom, but especially that which in the book of Scripture is elevated by the spirit of prophecy to the prefiguration of spiritual things. But more does the eternal wisdom appear in those creatures in whose likeness God wished to appear in angelic ministry. And most specially does it appear in those which He wished to institute for the purpose of signifying which are not only signs according to their common name but also Sacraments.

13. From all this it follows that the invisible things of God are clearly seen, from the creation of the world, being understood by the things that are made; so that those who are unwilling to give heed to them and to know God in them all, to bless Him and to love Him, are inexcusable [Rom., 1, 20], while they are unwilling to be carried forth from the shadows into the wonderful light of God [I Cor., 15, 57]. But thanks be to God through Jesus Christ our Lord, Who has transported us out of darkness into His wonderful light, when through these lights given from without we are disposed to re-enter into the mirror of our mind, in which the divine lights shine [I Peter, 2, 9].

CHAPTER THREE

OF THE REFLECTION OF GOD IN HIS IMAGE STAMPED UPON OUR NATURAL POWERS

1. The two steps mentioned above, by leading us to God by means of His Traces, whereby He shines forth in all creatures, have led us to the point of entering into ourselves, that is, into our minds in which the divine image shines. Now in the third place, as we enter into ourselves, as if leaving the vestibule and coming into the sanctum, that is, the outer part of the tabernacle, we should strive to see God through a mirror. In this mirror the light of truth is shining before our minds as in a candelabrum, for in it gleams the resplendent image of the most blessed Trinity.

Enter then into yourselves and see, for your mind loves itself most fervently. Nor could it love itself unless it knew itself. Nor would it know itself unless it remembered itself, for we receive nothing through intelligence which is not present to our memory. And from this be advised, not with the eye of the flesh but with that of reason, that your soul has a threefold power. Consider then the operations and the functions of these three powers, and you will be able to see God in yourselves as in an image, which is to see through a glass darkly [I Cor., 13, 12].

2. The operation of memory is retention and representation, not only of things present, corporeal, and temporal, but also of past and future things, simple and eternal. For memory retains the past by recalling it, the present by receiving it, the future by foreseeing it. It retains the simple, as the principles of continuous and discrete quantities—the point, the instant, the unit—without which it is impossible to remember or to think about those things whose source is in these. Nonetheless it retains the eternal principles and the axioms

22

of the sciences and retains them eternally. For it can never so forget them while it uses reason that it will not approve of them when heard and assent to them, not as though it were perceiving them for the first time, but as if it were recognizing them as innate and familiar, as appears when someone says to another, "One must either affirm or deny," or, "Every whole is greater than its part," or any other law which cannot be rationally contradicted.

From the first actual retention of all temporal things, namely, of the past, present, and future, it has the likeness of eternity whose indivisible present extends to all times. From the second it appears that it is not only formed from without by images [phantasms], but also by receiving simple forms from above and retaining them in itself—forms which cannot enter through the doors of the senses and the images of sensible things. From the third it follows that it has an undying light present to itself in which it remembers unchangeable truths. And thus, through the operations of the memory, it appears that the soul itself is the image of God and His likeness, so present to itself and having Him present that it receives Him in actuality and is susceptible of receiving Him in potency, and that it can also participate in Him.

3. The operation of the intellect is concerned with the meaning of terms, propositions, and inferences. The intellect, however, understands the meaning of terms when it comprehends what anything is through its definition. But a definition must be made by higher terms and these by still higher, until one comes to the highest and most general, in ignorance of which the lower cannot be defined. Unless, therefore, it is known what is Being-in-itself, the definition of no special substance can be fully known. Nor can Being-in-itself be known unless it be known along with its conditions: the one, the true, the good. Since being, however, can be known as incomplete or complete, as imperfect or perfect, as potential or actual, as relative or absolute, as partial or total, as transient or permanent, as dependent or independent, as mixed with non-being or as pure, as contingent or necessary

(*per se*), as posterior or prior, as mutable or immutable, as simple or composite; since privations and defects can be known only through affirmations in some positive sense, our intellect cannot reach the point of fully understanding any of the created beings unless it be favored by the understanding of the purest, most actual, most complete, and absolute Being, which is simply and eternally Being, and in which are the principles of all things in their purity. For how would the intellect know that a being is defective and incomplete if it had no knowledge of being free from all defect? And thus for all the aforesaid conditions.

The intellect is said to comprehend truly the meaning of propositions when it knows with certitude that they are true. And to know this is simply to know, since error is impossible in comprehension of this sort. For it knows that such truth cannot be otherwise than it is. It knows, therefore, that such truth is unchangeable. But since our mind itself is changeable, it cannot see that truth shining forth unchangeably except by some light shining without change in any way; and it is impossible that such a light be a mutable creature. Therefore it knows in that light which enlighteneth every man that cometh into this world [John, 1, 9], which is true light and the Word which in the beginning was with God [John, 1, 1].

Our intellect perceives truly the meaning of inference when it sees that a conclusion necessarily follows from its premises. This it sees not only in necessary terms but also in contingent. Thus if a man is running, a man is moving. It perceives, however, this necessary connection, not only in things which are, but also in things which are not. Thus if a man exists, it follows that if he is running, he is moved. And this is true even if the man is not existing. The necessity of this mode of inference comes not from the existence of the thing in matter, because that is contingent, nor from its existence in the soul, because then it would be a fiction if it were not in the world of things. Therefore it comes from the archetype in eternal art according to which things have an aptitude and a comportment toward one another by reason of the representation of that eternal art. As Augustine says in his *On True Religion* [Ch. 39, 72], "The light of all who reason truly is kindled at that truth and strives to return to it." From which it is obvious that our intellect is conjoined with that eternal truth so that it cannot receive anything with certainty except under its guidance. Therefore you can see the truth through yourself, the truth that teaches you, if concupiscence and phantasms do not impede you and place themselves like clouds between you and the rays of truth.

4. The operation of the power of choice is found in deliberation, judgment, and desire. Deliberation is found in inquiring what is better, this or that. But the better has no meaning except by its proximity to the best. But such proximity is measured by degrees of likeness. No one, therefore, can know whether this is better than that unless he knows that this is closer to the best. But no one knows that one of two things is more like another unless he knows the other. For I do not know that this man is like Peter unless I know or am acquainted with Peter. Therefore the idea of the good must be involved in every deliberation about the highest good.

Certain judgment of the objects of deliberation comes about through some law. But none can judge with certainty through law unless he be certain that that law is right and that he ought not to judge it. But the mind judges itself. Since, then, it cannot judge the law it employs in judging, that law is higher than our minds; and through this higher law one makes judgments according to the degree with which it is impressed upon it. But there is nothing higher than the human mind except Him Who made it. Therefore our deliberative faculty in judging reaches upward to divine laws if it solves its problems completely.

Now desire is of that which especially moves one. But that especially moves one which is especially loved. But happiness is loved above all. But happiness does not come about except through the best and ultimate end. Human desire, therefore, seeks nothing unless it be the highest good or something which leads to it or something which has some resemblance to it. So great is the force of the highest good that nothing can be loved except through desire for it by a creature which errs and is deceived when it takes truth's image and likeness for the truth.

See then how close the soul is to God and how memory in its operations leads to eternity, intelligence to truth, the power of choice to the highest goodness.

5. Following the order and origin and comportment of these powers, we are led to the most blessed Trinity itself. From memory arises intelligence as its offspring, for then do we know when a likeness which is in the memory leaps into the eye of the intellect, which is nothing other than a word. From memory and intelligence is breathed forth love, which is the tie between the two. These three—the generating mind, the word, and love—are in the soul as memory, intelligence, and will, which are consubstantial, coequal, and coeval, mutually immanent. If then God is perfect spirit, He has memory, intelligence, and will; and He has both the begotten Word and spirated Love. These are necessarily distinguished, since one is produced from the other—distinguished, not essentially or accidentally, but personally. When therefore the mind considers itself, it rises through itself as through a mirror to the contemplation of the Blessed Trinity—Father, Word, and Love—three persons coeternal, coequal, and consubstantial; so that each one is in each of the others, though one is not the other, but all three are one God.

6. This consideration which the soul has of its threefold and unified principle through the trinity of its powers, by which it is the image of God, is supported by the light of knowledge which perfects it and informs it, and represents in three ways the most blessed Trinity. For all philosophy is either natural or rational or moral. The first deals with the cause of being, and therefore leads to the power of the Father. The second deals with the principle of understanding, and therefore leads to the wisdom of the Word. The third deals with the order of living, and therefore leads to the goodness of the Holy Spirit.

Again, the first is divided into metaphysics, mathematics, and physics. The first concerns the essences of things; the second, numbers and figures; the third, natures, powers, and extensive operations. Therefore the first leads to the First Principle, the Father; the second, to His image, the Son; the third, to the gift of the Holy Spirit.

The second is divided into grammar, which gives us the power of expression; logic, which gives us skill in argumentation; rhetoric, which makes us skillful in persuasion or stirring the emotions. And this similarly images the mystery of the most blessed Trinity.

The third is divided into individual, family, and political [problems].[1] And therefore the first images the First Principle, which has no birth; the second, the family relationship of the Son; the third, the liberality of the Holy Spirit.

7. All these sciences have certain and infallible rules, like rays of light descending from the eternal law into our minds. And thus our minds, illumined and suffused by such great radiance, unless they be blind, can be led through themselves alone to the contemplation of that eternal light. The irradiation and consideration of this light holds the wise suspended in wonder; and, on the other hand, it leads into confusion the foolish, who do not believe that they may understand. Hence this prophecy is fulfilled: "Thou enlightenest wonderfully from the everlasting hills. All the foolish of heart were troubled" [Ps., 75, 5-6].

[1] In Latin, *monasticam, oeconomicam et politicam.*

CHAPTER FOUR

Of the Reflection of God in His Image Reformed by the Gifts of Grace

1. But since not only by passing through ourselves but also within ourselves is it given to us to contemplate the First Principle, and this is greater than the preceding, therefore this mode of thought reaches to the fourth level of contemplation. It seems amazing, however, when it is clear that God is so near to our minds, that there are so few who see the First Principle in themselves. But the reason is close at hand. For the human mind, distracted by cares, does not enter into itself through memory; obscured by phantasms, it does not return into itself through intelligence; allured by concupiscence, it never returns to itself through the desire for inner sweetness and spiritual gladness. Thus, lying totally in this sensible world, it cannot return to itself as to the image of God.

2. And since, when anyone lies fallen, he must remain there prostrate unless someone give a helping hand, and he falls in order to rise again [Isaiah, 24, 20], our soul has not been able to be raised perfectly from the things of sense to an intuition of itself and of the eternal Truth in itself unless the Truth, having assumed human form in Christ, should make itself into a ladder, repairing the first ladder which was broken in Adam.

Therefore, however much anyone is illuminated only by the light of nature and of acquired science, he cannot enter into himself that he may delight in the Lord in himself, unless Christ be his mediator, Who says, "I am the door. By me, if any man enter in, he shall be saved; and he shall go in, and go out, and shall find pastures" [John, 10, 9]. We do not, however, approach this door unless we believe in Him, hope in Him, and love Him. It is therefore necessary, if we wish to enter into the fruition of Truth, as into Paradise, that we enter through the faith, hope, and charity of the Mediator between God and man, Jesus Christ, Who is as the tree of life in the middle of Paradise.

3. The image of our mind must therefore be clothed also in the three theological virtues by which the soul is purified, illuminated, and perfected; and thus the image is repaired and is made like the heavenly Jerusalem and part of the Church militant, which, according to the Apostle, is the child of the heavenly Jerusalem. For he says: "But that Jerusalem which is above is free, which is our mother" [Gal., 4, 26]. Therefore the soul which believes in, hopes in, and loves Jesus Christ, Who is the Word incarnate, uncreated, and spirated, that is, the way and the truth and the life, when by faith he believes in Christ as in the uncreated Word, which is the Word and the splendor of the Father, he recovers spiritual hearing and vision: hearing to receive the lessons of Christ, vision to look upon the splendor of His light. When, however, he yearns with hope to receive the spirated Word, through desire and affection he recovers spiritual olfaction. When he embraces the incarnate Word in charity, as one receiving from Him delight and passing into Him through ecstatic love, he recovers taste and touch. When these senses are recovered, when he sees his spouse and hears, smells, tastes, and embraces Him, he can sing like the Bride a Canticle of Canticles, as was done on the occasion of this fourth stage of contemplation, which no one knoweth but he that receiveth it [Apoc., 2, 17]. For it occurs in affective experience rather than in rational consideration. On this level, when the inner senses are renewed in order to perceive the highest beauty, to hear the highest harmony, smell the highest fragrance, taste the highest delicacy, apprehend the highest delights, the soul is disposed to mental elevation through devotion, wonder, and exultation, in accordance with those three exclamations which are in the Canticle of Canticles. Of these the first arises from

the abundance of devotion, by which the soul becomes like
a pillar of smoke of aromatic spices, of myrrh and frankin-
cense [Cant., 3, 6]; the second, from the excellence of wonder,
by which the soul becomes as the dawn, the moon, and the
sun, like the series of illuminations which suspend the soul
in wonder as it considers its spouse; the third, from the superabundance of exultation, by which the soul, overflowing with
the sweetest delight, leans totally upon its beloved [Cant., 8, 5].

4. When this is accomplished, our spirit is made hierarchical to mount upward through its conformity to the heavenly
Jerusalem, into which no one enters unless through grace it
has descended into his heart, as John saw in his Apocalypse
[21, 2]. But then it descends into one's heart when, by the
reformation of the image through the theological virtues and
through the delights of the spiritual senses and ecstatic elevation, our spirit has been made hierarchical, that is, purged,
illuminated, and perfected. Likewise the soul is stamped by
the following nine steps when it is disposed in an orderly way:
perception, deliberation, self-impulsion, ordination, strength-
ening, command, reception, divine illumination, union,[1]
which one by one correspond to the nine orders of angels, so
that the first three stages correspond to nature in the human
mind, the next three to industry, and the last three to grace.[2]
With these acquired, the soul, entering into itself, enters into
the heavenly Jerusalem, where, considering the orders of the
angels, it sees God in them, Who living in them causes all
their operations. Whence Bernard said to Eugenius that—

God in the seraphim loves as Charity, in the Cherubim He
knows as Truth, in the Thrones He is seated as Equity, in the

---

[1] Reading *unitio* instead of *unctio*.

[2] The translation of the names of the nine steps is based on St. Bonaventura's *Hexaemeron*, XXII, 25-27, where each is explained. Since they
are somewhat awkward in English, I give the Latin equivalents
in order. They are so similar to English words that the student who wishes
may retain them in transliteration in place of my rendering. They run:
*nuntiatio, dictatio, ductio, ordinatio, roboratio, imperatio, susceptio,
revelatio, unctio* (or *unitio*, if my reading be acceptable).

Dominations He dominates as Majesty, in the Principalities He rules as the First Principle, in the Powers He watches over us as Salvation, in the Virtues He operates as Virtue, in the Archangels He reveals as Light, in the Angels He aids as Piety.[3]

From all of which God is seen to be all in all through the contemplation of Him in the minds in which He dwells through the gifts of His overflowing Charity.

5. For this grade of contemplation there is especially and outstandingly added as a support the consideration of Holy Scripture divinely issued, as philosophy was added to the preceding. For Holy Scripture is principally concerned with the works of reparation. Wherefore it especially deals with faith, hope, and charity, by which the soul is reformed, and most of all with charity. Concerning this the Apostle says that the end of the Commandments is reached by a pure heart and a good conscience and an unfeigned faith [I Tim., 1, 5]. This is the fulfillment of the Law, as he says. And our Saviour adds that all the Law and the Prophets depend upon these two Commandments: the love of God and of one's neighbor. Which two are united in the one spouse of the Church, Jesus Christ, Who is at once neighbor and God, at once brother and Lord, at once king and friend, at once Word uncreated and incarnate, our maker and remaker, the alpha and omega. He is the highest hierarch, purging and illuminating and perfecting His spouse, the whole Church and any holy soul.

6. Of this hierarch and this ecclesiastical hierarchy is the entire Holy Scripture by which we are taught to be purified, illuminated, and perfected, and this according to the triple law handed down to us in it: the law of Nature, of Scripture, and of Grace; or rather according to the triple principal part of it: the Mosaic Law purifying, the prophetic revelation illuminating, and evangelical teaching perfecting; or above all, according to the triple spiritual meaning of it—the tropological which purifies us for an honest life, the allegorical which illuminates us for the clarity of understanding, the

[3] St. Bernard of Clairvaux to Pope Eugenius III.

analogical which perfects us by mental elevation and the most delightful perceptions of wisdom—in accordance with the three aforesaid theological virtues and the spiritual senses reformed and the three above-mentioned stages of elevation and hierarchical acts of the mind, by.which our mind retreats into itself so that it may look upon God in the brightness of the saints [Ps., 109, 3] and in them, as in a chamber, it may sleep in peace and take its rest [Ps., 4, 9] while the spouse adjures it that it stir not up till she pleases [Cant., 2, 7].

7. Now from these two middle steps, by which we proceed to contemplate God within ourselves as in the mirrors of created images—and this as with wings opened for flying which hold the middle place—we can understand that we are led into the divine by the powers of the rational soul itself placed therein by nature as far as their operations, habits, and knowledge are concerned, as appears from the third stage. For we are led by the powers of the soul reformed by virtues freely granted, by the spiritual senses, and by mental elevation, as appears from the fourth stage. We are nonetheless led through hierarchical operations, that is, by purgation, illumination, and perfection of human minds through the hierarchical revelations of the Holy Scriptures given to us, according to the Apostle, through the Angels in the hand of a mediator [Gal., 3, 19]. And finally we are led by hierarchies and hierarchical orders which are found to be ordered in our minds in the likeness of the heavenly Jerusalem.

8. Our mind, filled with all these intellectual illuminations, is inhabited by the divine wisdom as the house of God; become the daughter, the spouse, and the friend of God; made a member of Christ the head, the sister, and the fellow-heir; made nonetheless the temple of the Holy Spirit, founded by faith, elevated by hope, and dedicated to God by the sanctity of the mind and the body. All of this has been brought about by the most sincere love of Christ which is poured forth into our hearts by the Holy Spirit, Who is given to us [Rom., 5, 5], without which Spirit we cannot know the secrets of God. For just as no one can know the things of a man except the spirit

of a man that is in him, so the things also that are of God
no man knoweth but the spirit of God [I Cor., 2, 11]. In
charity then let us be rooted and founded, that we may be
able to comprehend with all the saints what is the length of
eternity, the breadth of liberality, the height of majesty, and
the depth of the wisdom which judges us [Eph., 3, 17-18].

CHAPTER FIVE

OF THE REFLECTION OF THE DIVINE UNITY IN ITS PRIMARY NAME WHICH IS BEING

1. It happens that we may contemplate God not only outside of us but also within us and above us. [Thus we contemplate Him] outside through His traces, inside through His image, and above us through His light, which has signed upon our minds the light of eternal Truth, since the mind itself is immediately formed by Truth itself. Those who exercise themselves in the first manner have already entered into the atrium of the tabernacle; the second have entered into the sanctum; but the third have entered into the Holy of Holies with the High Priest, the Holy of Holies where above the ark are the Cherubim of glory overshadowing the propitiatory. By these modes we understand two ways or degrees of contemplation of the invisible and eternal things of God, of which one deals with God's essential attributes, the other with the properties of the Persons.

2. The first way first and foremost signifies Him in Being itself, saying *He Who Is* is the primary name of God. The second signifies Him in His goodness, saying this [goodness] is the primary name of God. The former refers above all to the Old Testament, which preaches the unity of the divine essence, whence it was said to Moses, "I am Who I am." The second refers to the New Testament, which lays down the plurality of the Persons, by baptizing in the name of the Father and of the Son and of the Holy Spirit. Therefore our Master Christ, wishing to elevate the youth who had served the law to evangelical perfection, attributed the name of goodness principally and precisely to God. No one, He said, is good but God alone [Luke, 18, 19]. Damascenus [*De fide orthod.*, 1, 9]

therefore, following Moses, says that *He Who Is* is the primary name of God. Dionysius, following Christ, says that *goodness* is God's primary name.

3. If you wish then to contemplate the invisible traits of God in so far as they belong to the unity of His essence, fix your gaze upon Being itself, and see that Being is most certain in itself; for it cannot be thought not to be, since the purest Being occurs only in full flight from Non-Being, just as nothingness is in full flight from Being. Therefore, just as the utterly nothing contains nought of Being nor of its conditions, so contrariwise Being itself contains no Non-Being, neither in actuality nor in potency, neither in matters of fact nor in our thinking. Since, however, Non-Being is the privation of Being, it cannot enter the intellect except through Being; Being, however, cannot enter through anything other than itself. For everything which is thought of is either thought of as Non-Being or as Being-in-potency or as Being-in-actuality. If, therefore, Non-Being is intelligible only through Being, and if Being-in-potency can be understood only through Being-in-actuality, and if Being is the name of that pure actuality of Being, Being then is what first enters the intellect, and that Being is pure actuality. But this is not particular Being, which is restricted Being, since that is mixed with potentiality. Nor is this analogous Being, for such has a minimum of actuality since it has only a minimum of being. It remains, therefore, that that Being is divine Being.

4. Marvelous then is the blindness of the intellect which does not consider that which is its primary object and without which it can know nothing. But just as the eye intent upon the various differences of the colors does not see the light by which it sees the other things and, if it sees it, does not notice it, so the mind's eye, intent upon particular and universal beings, does not notice Being itself, which is beyond all genera, though that comes first before the mind and through it all other things. Wherefore it seems very true that just as the bat's eye behaves in the light, so the eye of the mind behaves before the most obvious things of nature. Because accustomed to the

shadows of beings and the phantasms of the sensible world, when it looks upon the light of the highest Being, it seems to see nothing, not understanding that darkness itself is the fullest illumination of the mind [Ps., 138, 11], just as when the eye sees pure light it seems to itself to be seeing nothing.

5. See then purest Being itself, if you can, and you will understand that it cannot be thought of as derivative from another. And thus necessarily that must be thought of as absolutely primal which can be derivative neither from nothing nor from anything. For what exists through itself if Being does not exist through itself and of itself? You will understand that, lacking Non-Being in every respect and therefore having no beginning nor end, it is eternal. You will understand also that it contains nothing in itself save Being itself, for it is in no way composite, but is most simple. You will understand that it has no potentialities within it, since every possible has in some way something of Non-Being, but Being is the highest actuality. You will understand that it has no defect, for it is most perfect. Finally, you will understand that it has no diversity, for it is One in the highest degree.

Being, therefore, which is pure Being and most simply Being and absolutely Being, is Being primary, eternal, most simple, most actual, most perfect, and one to the highest degree.

6. And these things are so certain that Being itself cannot be thought of by an intellect as opposed to these, and one of these traits implies the others. For since it is simply Being, therefore it is simply primary; because it is simply primary, therefore it is not made from another nor from itself, and therefore it is eternal. Likewise, since it is primary and eternal, and therefore not from others, it is therefore most simple. Furthermore, since it is primary, eternal, and most simple, therefore it contains no potentiality mixed with actuality, and therefore it is most actual. Likewise, since it is primary, eternal, most simple, most actual, it is most perfect. To such a Being nothing is lacking, nor can anything be added. Since it is primary, eternal, most simple, most actual, most perfect, it is therefore one to the highest degree. For what is predicated

because of its utter superabundance is applicable to all things. For what is simply predicated because of superabundance cannot possibly be applied to anything but the one.[1] Wherefore, if God is the name of the primary, eternal, most simple, most actual, most perfect Being, it is impossible that He be thought of as not being nor as anything save One alone. "Hear, O Israel, the Lord our God is one God." If you see this in the pure simplicity of your mind, you will somehow be infused with the illumination of eternal light.

7. But you have ground for rising in wonder. For Being itself is first and last, is eternal and yet most present, is simplest and greatest, is most actual and immutable, is perfect and immense, is most highly one and yet all-inclusive. If you wonder over these things with a pure mind, while you look further, you will be infused with a greater light, until you finally see that Being is last because it is first. For since it is first, it produces all things for its own sake alone; and therefore it must be the very end, the beginning and the consummation, the alpha and the omega. Therefore it is most present because it is eternal. For since it is eternal, it does not come from another; nor does it cease to be nor pass from one thing to another, and therefore has no past nor future but only present being. Therefore it is greatest because most simple. For since it is most simple in essence, therefore it is greatest in power; because power, the more greatly it is unified, the closer it is to the infinite. Therefore it is most immutable, because most actual. For that which is most actual is therefore pure act. And as such it acquires nothing new nor does it lose what it had, and therefore cannot be changed. Therefore it is most immense, because most perfect. For since it is most perfect, nothing can be thought of which is better, nobler, or more worthy. And on this account there is nothing greater. And every such thing is immense. Therefore it is all-inclusive (*omnimodal*), because it is one to the highest degree. For that

---

[1] The editors of the Latin text cite this as a quotation from Aristotle's *Topics*, V. 5, but I have not been able to find the passage which might be the source of it.

which is one to the highest degree is the universal source of all multiplicity. And for this reason it is the universal efficient cause of all things, the exemplary and the final cause, as the cause of Being, the principle of intelligibility, the order of living.[2] And therefore it is all-inclusive, not as the essence of all things, but as the superexcellent and most universal and most sufficient cause of all essences, whose power, because most highly unified in essence, is therefore most highly infinite and most fertile in efficacy.

8. Recapitulating, let us say: Because, then, Being is most pure and absolute, that which is Being simply is first and last and, therefore, the origin and the final cause of all. Because eternal and most present, therefore it encompasses and penetrates all duration, existing at once as their center and circumference. Because most simple and greatest, therefore it is entirely within and entirely without all things and, therefore, is an intelligible sphere whose center is everywhere and whose circumference nowhere. Because most actual and most immutable, then "remaining stable it causes the universe to move" [Boethius, *Cons.* III, met. 9]. Because most perfect and immense, therefore within all, though not included in them; beyond all, but not excluded from them; above all, but not transported beyond them; below all, and yet not cast down beneath them. Because most highly one and all-inclusive, therefore all in all, although all things are many and it is only one. And this is so since through most simple unity, clearest truth, and most sincere goodness there is in it all power, all exemplary causality, and all communicability. And therefore from it and by it and in it are all things. And this is so since it is omnipotent, omniscient, and all-good. And to see this perfectly is to be blessed. As was said to Moses, "I will show thee all good" [Exod. 33, 19].

---

[2] In Latin: *causa essendi, ratio intelligendi, et ordo vivendi.*

CHAPTER SIX

Of the Reflection of the Most Blessed Trinity in Its Name, Which Is Good

1. After a consideration of the essential traits [of God], the eye of the intelligence must be raised to look upon the most Blessed Trinity, in order that the second Cherub may be placed next to the first. Just as Being is the root and name of the vision of the essential traits, so Good is the principal foundation of our contemplation of the divine emanations [of the Trinity].

2. See then and pay heed, since the best which exists simply is that than which nothing better can be thought of. And this is such that it cannot be rightly thought not to be. For Being is in all ways better than Non-Being. This is such that it cannot rightly be thought of unless conceived of as both three and one. For the Good is said to be self-diffusive. The highest good is therefore the most self-diffusive. The greatest diffusion, however, can exist only if it is actual and intrinsic, substantial and hypostatic, natural and voluntary, free and necessary, lacking nothing and perfect. Unless, then, there be eternally in the *highest good* a production which is actual and consubstantial, and an hypostasis as noble as the producer through generation and spiration, so that it would be from the eternal principle eternally co-producing and would be beloved (*dilectus*) in itself and co-loved (*condilectus*), generated, and spirated as are the Father and the Son and the Holy Spirit, in no way would it be the highest good, for it would not diffuse itself most highly. For temporal diffusion in creation is nothing else than central and punctiform with respect to the immensity of the eternal goodness. Whence also can some diffusion be conceived as greater than that—to wit, that in which the diffusive power communicates its whole substance

39

and nature to another. Therefore the highest good would not exist if it could lack that characteristic either in existence or in thought.

If then you can look with the mind's eye upon the purity of goodness, which is the pure actualization of the principle of Charity, pouring forth free and due love, and both mingled together, which is the fullest diffusion according to nature and will—the diffusion as Word, in which all things are expressed, and as Gift, in which all other gifts are given—you may see by the highest communicability of the Good that a Trinity of Father and Son and Holy Spirit is necessary. Because of the greatest goodness, it is necessary that there be in them the greatest communicability, and out of the greatest communicability the greatest consubstantiality, and from the greatest consubstantiality the greatest configurability, and from all these the greatest coequality; and therefore the greatest co-eternity as well as, because of all the aforesaid, the greatest co-intimacy, by which one is in the other necessarily through the highest degree of mutual penetration and one operates with the other through the complete identity of substances and power and operation of the most Blessed Trinity itself.

3. But when you contemplate these things, see that you do not think yourself able to understand the incomprehensible. For you have still in these six stages to consider what most strongly leads our mind's eye into the stupor of wonder. For there [in the Trinity] is the greatest communicability with individuality of the persons, the greatest consubstantiality with plurality of the hypostases, the greatest configurability with distinct personality, the greatest co-equality with order, the greatest co-eternity with emanation, the greatest mutual intimacy with mission. Who in the face of such great marvels would not start in wonder? But we understand with greatest certitude that all these exist in the most Blessed Trinity if we raise our eyes to the goodness that excels all goodness. For if there is the greatest communication and true diffusion, there is also true origin and true distinction. And because the whole and not the part is communicated, therefore it is itself given

as a whole and not as a part. Therefore the one emanating and the one producing are distinguished by their properties, and yet are essentially one. Since, then, they are distinguished by their properties, therefore they have personal properties and a plurality of hypostases and an emanation of origin and an order which is not of posteriority but of origin, and a mission not of local change but of free spiration, because of the authority of the producer which every sender has in respect to that which is sent. Because they are substantially one, therefore it must be true that there is unity in essence and in form, in dignity and in eternity, in existence and illimitability. While therefore you consider these things one by one in themselves, you have a reason for contemplating the truth; when you compare them with one another, you have the wherewithal to hover in highest wonder; and therefore, that your mind may ascend in wonder to wonderful contemplation, these things should be considered all together.

4. For these Cherubim signify this also, since they look at each other. Nor is this free from mystery, that they look toward each, their faces being turned toward the propitiatory [Exod., 25, 20], that there may be verified what the Lord said in John, "Now this is the eternal life: That they may know thee, the only true God, and Jesus Christ, Whom thou hast sent" [John, 17, 3]. For we should wonder not only at the essential and personal traits of God in themselves, but also in comparison with the superwonderful union of God and man in the unity of Christ's person.

5. For if you are the Cherub when you contemplate the essentials of God and you wonder because the divine Being is at once primary and last Being, eternal and most present, most simple and greatest or unlimited, all everywhere and yet never bounded, most actual and never moved, most perfect and having nothing superfluous or lacking, and yet immense and infinite without bounds, one to the highest degree and yet all-inclusive as having all things in itself, as total power, total truth, total goodness, look to the propitiatory and wonder that in it the primal principle is joined to the last term, God

joined with man formed on the sixth day, the eternal joined with temporal man, born in the fullness of time of a Virgin—the most simple joined with the most composite, the most actual with the most passive and mortal, the most perfect and immense with the little, the most highly unified and all-inclusive with the composite individual distinct from all else, namely, Jesus Christ.

6. If, however, you are the other Cherub when you contemplate the properties of the Persons, you will also wonder that communicability exists with individuality, consubstantiality with plurality, configurability with personality, co-equality with order, co-eternity with production, co-intimacy with mission, for the Son was sent by the Father, and the Holy Spirit by both, Who nevertheless is always with Them and never withdraws from Them. Look to the propitiatory and wonder because in Christ is a personal union with a trinity of substances and a duality of natures, an absolute agreement with a plurality of wills, a common speech between God and man with plurality of properties, an equal worship with plurality of ranks, an equal exaltation above all things with plurality of dignities, a condominium with plurality of powers.

7. In this consideration is the perfection of the mind's illumination, when, as if on the sixth day, it sees man made in the image of God. If then the image is an express likeness when our mind contemplates in Christ the Son of God, Who is the natural image of the invisible God, our humanity now wonderfully exalted, now ineffably united, by seeing at once in one Being the first and the last, the highest and the lowest, the circumference and the center, the alpha and the omega, the caused and the cause, the creator and the creature, the book written within and without, it [the mind] arrives at a perfect being in order that it may arrive with God at the perfection of His illuminations on the sixth level, as if on the sixth day; nor does anything more remain save the day of rest, on which, by the elevation of the mind, its insight rests from all work which He had done.

CHAPTER SEVEN

OF MENTAL AND MYSTICAL ELEVATION, IN WHICH REPOSE IS GIVEN TO THE INTELLECT WHEN THE AFFECTIONS PASS ENTIRELY INTO GOD THROUGH ELEVATION

1. Now that these six considerations have been studied as the six steps of the true throne of Solomon by which one ascends to peace, where the truly peaceful man reposes in peace of mind as if in the inner Jerusalem; as if, again, on the six wings of the Cherub by which the mind of the truly contemplative man grows strong to rise again, filled with the illumination of supreme wisdom; as if, once again, during the first six days in which the mind has to be exercised that it may finally arrive at the Sabbath of rest after it has beheld God outside itself through His traces and in His traces, within itself by His image and in His image, above itself by the likeness of the divine light shining down upon us and in that light, in so far as is possible in this life and the exercise of our mind—when, finally, on the sixth level we have come to the point of beholding in the first and highest principle and the Mediator of God and men, Jesus Christ, those things of which the likeness cannot in any wise be found in creatures and which exceed all the insight of the human intellect, there remains that by looking upon these things it [the mind] rise on high and pass beyond not only this sensible world but itself also. In this passage Christ is the way and the door, Christ is the stairway and the vehicle, like the propitiatory over the ark of God and the mystery which has been hidden from eternity [Eph., 3, 9].

2. He who with full face looks to this propitiatory by look-

43

ing upon Him suspended on the cross in faith, hope, and charity, in devotion, wonder, exultation, appreciation, praise, and jubilation, makes a passover—that is, the phase or passage [Exod., 12, 11] with Him—that he may pass over the Red Sea by the staff of the cross from Egypt into the Desert, where he may taste the hidden manna and with Christ may rest in the tomb as if outwardly dead, yet knowing, as far as possible in our earthly condition, what was said on the cross to the thief cleaving to Christ: "Today thou shalt be with me in Paradise."

3. That was shown to the blessed Francis when, in the transport of contemplation on the high mountain—where I thought out these things which I have written—there appeared to him the Seraph with the six wings nailed to the cross, as I and several others have heard from the companion who was with him when he passed over into God through the transports of contemplation and became the example of perfect contemplation, just as previously he had been of action; as another Jacob is changed into Israel, so through him all truly spiritual men have been invited by God to passage of this kind and to mental transport by example rather than by word.

4. In this passage, if it is perfect, all intellectual operations should be abandoned, and the whole height of our affection should be transferred and transformed into God. This, however, is mystical and most secret, which no man knoweth but he that hath received it [Apoc., 2, 17], nor does he receive it unless he desire it; nor does he desire it unless the fire of the Holy Spirit, Whom Christ sent to earth, has inflamed his marrow. And therefore the Apostle says that this mystic wisdom is revealed through the Holy Spirit.

5. Since, therefore, nature is powerless in this matter and industry but slightly able, little should be given to inquiry but much to unction, little to the tongue but much to inner joy, little to the word and to writings and all to the gift of God, that is, to the Holy Spirit, little or nothing to creation and all to the creative essence, Father, Son, and Holy Spirit, saying with Dionysius to God the Trinity:

Trinity, superessential and superdivine and supergood guardian of Christian knowledge of God, direct thou us into the more-than-unknown and superluminous and most sublime summit of mystical eloquence, where new and absolute and unchangeable mysteries of theology are deeply hidden, according to the superluminous darkness of instructive silence—darkness which is supermanifest and superresplendent, and in which all is aglow, pouring out upon the invisible intellects the splendors of invisible goodness.[2]

This to God. To the friend, however, to whom I address this book, let me say with the same Dionysius:

Thou then, my friend, if thou desirest mystic visions, with strengthened feet abandon thy senses and intellectual operations, and both sensible and invisible things, and both all non-being and being; and unknowingly restore thyself to unity as far as possible, unity of Him Who is above all essence and knowledge. And when thou hast transcended thyself and all things in immeasurable and absolute purity of mind, thou shalt ascend to the superessential rays of divine shadows, leaving all behind and freed from ties of all.[3]

6. If you should ask how these things come about, question grace, not instruction; desire, not intellect; the cry of prayer, not pursuit of study; the spouse, not the teacher; God, not man; darkness, not clarity; not light, but the wholly flaming fire which will bear you aloft to God with fullest unction and burning affection. This fire is God, and the furnace of this fire leadeth to Jerusalem; and Christ the man kindles it in the fervor of His burning Passion, which he alone truly perceives who says, "My soul rather chooseth hanging and my bones death" [Job, 7, 15]. He who chooses this death can see God because this is indubitably true: "Man shall not see me and live" [Exod., 33, 20]. Let us then die and pass over into darkness; let us impose silence on cares, concupiscence, and phantasms; let us pass over with the crucified Christ from this world to the Father [John, 13, 1], so that when the Father

---

[2] *Mystic Theology,* Ch. I [Migne, *Pat. Graec.,* Vol. III, 997].
[3] *Ibid.*

is shown to us we may say with Philip, "It is enough for us" [John, 14, 8]; let us hear with Paul, "My grace is sufficient for thee" [II Cor., 12, 9]; let us exult with David, saying, "For Thee my flesh and my heart hath fainted away; Thou art the God of my heart, and the God that is my portion forever [Ps., 72, 26]. . . . Blessed be the Lord God of Israel from everlasting to everlasting; and let all the people say: So be it, so be it" [Ps., 105, 48]. AMEN.

The Library of Liberal Arts

(Complete list sent upon request)

The Library of Liberal Arts

Aristotle: *On the Art of Poetry*

With a Supplement: *Aristotle on Music*. Translated by S. H. Butcher; translation corrected and edited, with an Introduction, by Milton C. Nahm. ("On Music" being part of *Politics*, translated by Benjamin Jowett) (6)   40 cents

H. Bergson: *An Introduction to Metaphysics*

Translated by T. E. Hulme. With an Introduction by Thomas A. Goudge (10)   35 cents

Bradley: *Ethical Studies (Selected Essays)*

With an Introduction by Ralph C. Ross. Contains: Why Should I Be Moral?; Pleasure for Pleasure's Sake; Duty for Duty's Sake; My Station and Its Duties; Concluding Remarks (28). *Cloth ed.* $1.80   80 cents

J. Butler: *Five Sermons*

With an Introduction by Stuart M. Brown, Jr. Contains: Preface (abridged); Sermons I, II, III, XI, and XII; Dissertation upon the Nature of Virtue (entire) (21)   50 cents

Calvin: *God and Political Duty*

With an Introduction by John T. McNeill. Contains: (from the *Institutes*) Dedication to Francis I; On Christian Liberty; On Civil Government; and related texts (23)   50 cents

Dante: *On World Government (De Monarchia)*

A new translation by Herbert W. Schneider. With an Introduction by Dino Bigongiari (15)   40 cents

Descartes: *Discourse on Method*

A new translation, with an Introduction, by Laurence J. Lafleur (19)   40 cents

————*Meditations*

A new translation, with an Introduction, by Laurence J. Lafleur (29)   50 cents

R. W. Emerson: *Nature*

With an Introduction by Joseph L. Blau (2)   35 cents

Epictetus: *Enchiridion*

Translated by T. W. Higginson. With an Introduction by Albert Salomon (8)   35 cents

Hegel: *Reason in History. A General Introduction to the Philosophy of World History*

A new translation, with an introduction, by Robert S. Hartman   75 cents

Hesiod: *Theogony*

A new translation, with an Introduction, by Norman O. Brown (36)   50 cents

Hume: *Political Essays*

With an Introduction by Charles W. Hendel. Contains: "Of the Origin of Justice and Property" and 17 selected essays (most of them entire) from *Essays, Moral, Political, and Literary* (34)   75 cents

(*Continued on inside cover*)

THE LIBERAL ARTS PRESS, INC.
153 W. 72nd Street, New York 23, N. Y.